Cognitive Behavioral Therapy

Your Ultimate Guide to Overcoming Anxiety, Depression, and Low Self-Esteem and Taking Control of Your Life

Jane Clarke

TABLE OF CONTENTS

ACKNOWLEDGMENTS

How often do we rely on reviews to find an interesting book that's worth our time and attention?

My Dear Reader! When I was writing my book, I put quite an effort to give you the maximum information and the tools that can be useful for everyone to understand what the « Cognitive Behavioral Therapy».

The only thing I want is that my pieces of advice would help as many people as possible and would reach everybody's mind and heart.

That's why Your opinion is extremely important for me and the others. Please, share thoughts and feelings that my book raises in You (just leave a review on the site Amazon). Moreover, if you have any questions or remarks, then contact me clarke.jane1309@gmail.com

I'll be incredibly happy to receive your feedback, my Dear Reader!

Faithfully yours,

Jane Clarke.

INTRODUCTION

Do you or your loved one struggle with depression, anxiety, addictions, eating disorder or phobias of any kind? Do you want to deal with these problems? Have you ever heard of Cognitive Behavioral Therapy (CBT)? Do you know that this technique can help you deal with these problems?

Well, the truth is, CBT is a short-term technique that is focused on helping people to deal with specific problems. As you go through treatment using this technique, you will be able to learn ways in which you can identify destructive thought patterns. You will also learn how you can change these patterns so that they do not have a negative influence on both your emotions and behavior.

The development of CBT has, in effect, revolutionized the treatment of depression by mainly focusing on how people think of themselves and how they respond to events from their surroundings. For example, if you think about road accidents long enough, you may end up avoiding road travels altogether.

This does not have to be. The main aim of CBT is to help you understand that you cannot control every aspect of taking place in our surroundings. However, you have the power to control how you interpret and handle the events in your environment. You have to realize that allowing those thoughts to control your decisions, emotions, and behavior can make the situation worse for you and the people around you.

You may be thinking, 'But these thoughts are spontaneous, I don't have anything to do with changing them.' Well, the truth is, they may be spontaneous, but you do not have to allow them to get the best of you. You do not have to accept them as true.

CBT will help you examine every thought that comes to mind so that you identify the evidence from reality that will either disqualify or support these thoughts. In so doing, you will be able to take a more realistic and objective look at the thoughts, and hence, your contribution to what you feel.

In other words, when you are aware of the negative, more unrealistic thoughts that dampen your emotions and behavior, you will start engaging in healthier patterns of thought and behavior.

So, what are you waiting for? Come with me and let's delve deeper into the subject of cognitive behavioral therapy.

1 CHAPTER

WHAT IS COGNITIVE BEHAVIORAL THERAPY?

This is one of the questions that so many people ask, whether they have a specific problem or not. Well, Cognitive Behavioral Therapy (CBT) can be defined as an effective technique that combines talk therapy with behavioral therapy. In other words, it is a type of psychotherapy that involves patients reframing their negative thought patterns into positive thought patterns.

When you transform your thoughts, you will ultimately realize positive outcomes in your actions and behaviors whenever you are experiencing challenging situations. This technique is very useful if you are struggling with such conditions as depression, anxiety, and eating disorders, among other problems.

The good thing with this technique is that when you are in the middle of therapy, you have the opportunity to work hand in hand with your therapist so that you can identify the source of your negative thoughts. This is the best way in which you can transform these negative thoughts into positive ones, and hence, ultimately grow a positive mindset.

One thing that you have to understand with CBT is that the main goal is for you to replace those negative thoughts and behaviors with productive ones. Ask yourself 'Are these thoughts bringing out the best in me? Are my actions causing me more harm than good?' When you try to evaluate the impact that these feelings have on you and the people around you, you will be able to use CBT to equip yourself to overcome difficult moments.

In other words, you will use the technique to recognize how your thoughts influence your emotions. You will simply establish a rather personalized mechanism that will help you cope with the real-world-situation.

2 CHAPTER

HOW DOES CBT WORK?

Well, so many people think that this technique is difficult, but trust me, it is one of the simplest ways in which you can overcome your problem. It works by helping you make sense of overwhelming issues by simply breaking them down into five major parts, namely:

- Situations
- Thoughts
- Emotions
- Feelings
- Actions

These five parts form the major concepts that underlie CBT. They are interconnected with each other and hence affect one another. For instance, when you face a particular situation, you begin to fuel thoughts about it, and this affects the way you feel; emotionally and physically. These feelings begin to take control of your physical body and hence influence how you act in response to the situation.

So many people wonder how this technique is different from other psychotherapies. Well, CBT is more pragmatic in the sense that it helps people identify the problems that they have and then helps them address them. It is also structured in that, instead of you talking about your life openly, you work with your therapist to discuss specific problems and then set goals for you to achieve while at it.

Additionally, CBT, unlike other psychotherapies, is focused mainly on the current problem. In other words, rather than trying to address issues that happened in the past, it aims at your thought process and your actions in response to them. In this case, the therapist will not tell you what to do, but they will work with you to identify solutions to your problems.

Using CBT to stop negative thought cycles

Did you know that there are helpful and unhelpful ways of reacting to a situation? Did you also know that your thoughts affect how you react to a situation?

Let us consider an example: *if your marriage ends in divorce, the chances of you thinking you are the one to blame are high. You may even begin to think that you are not capable of a meaningful relationship. These thoughts might get the best of you and make you feel hopeless, depressed, lonely, and fed up. You then stop going out and hence, shutter your chances of meeting new people. You simply get trapped in a negative cycle where you feel bad for and about yourself.*

Instead of accepting these thoughts, you should see your situation like any other marriage that has ended. Take that moment to reflect on what happened and learn from your mistakes and that of your partner. This way, you will not only come to terms with what has happened but also feel optimistic about the future. It is this kind of optimism that will fuel the social cues that will help you interact more with new people and better yourself.

Maybe your situation is not about divorce. It could be that you lost your job, closed your business or are facing some other problem. What you have to remember is that if you allow negative thoughts to cloud your mind, you will get trapped in negative feelings, sensations, and actions. This negative cycle will fuel new situations that will make you feel worse than you already do.

With CBT, you can stop these negative thoughts by simply breaking down that situation that is making you feel bad, scared or even anxious. In other words, it makes the whole situation manageable. It helps you transform each of these parts from negative patterns to positive ones, hence improve how you feel. It will help you transition from working with a therapist to working on your own in addressing problems you face every day with a high degree of success.

Exposure therapy

This is one form of CBT that is particularly aimed at helping people with the obsessive-compulsive disorder to deal with their issues. In this case, you have to bear in mind that talking about your problem is not very helpful. What is important is for you to learn to face your fears in a rather structured and methodical way through exposure.

You have to start with the things that bring you anxiety, but choose one that you can handle most easily. You then stay in this situation for an hour or two or until the time when you feel your fears and anxiety subsiding for a long while.

Most therapists insist on you repeating these exercises of exposure for at least three times each day. What is interesting is that, when you start facing your fears often, that anxiety begins to decline rather than increase, and will not last for very long.

You will then begin to gradually move to a more difficult situation. Then continue with the process until you have tackled all the things and situations that cause you panic and anxiety.

CBT Session

You can take part in a one-on-one session with your therapist or in a group of people dealing with the same issues as you are. If you choose to have a session with your therapist alone, you will have at least 5-20 sessions per week or fortnight. Every session will last from half-an-hour to one hour.

If you go through exposure therapy, one thing that you have to understand is that the sessions might be longer. The main aim of this is to ensure that you deal with anxiety hands-on so that it reduces by the end of every session. This may be in the clinic, outdoors, especially if you have specific fears, or in your home, especially if you have agoraphobia or OCD that involves certain items in your home.

What is important is for you to ensure that you are working with a professional who is trained in CBT. This can be a mental health nurse, psychiatrist or a psychologist.

Your first session

Before you can get all warmed up, the first thing is to determine whether CBT is the right mode of treatment for you. This upfront check ensures that you are comfortable during the process. In this case, your therapist will ask you a series of simple questions concerning your life and background.

In cases where you are struggling with anxiety or depression, it is important that you openly let your therapist know whether your issue interferes with your family, work and/or social life. You should also let them know about the events that you think are related to the problem, whether you have had treatment before and the objectives that you would like to achieve with the therapy.

If the CBT sessions are appropriate for you, it is important that you learn from your therapist what to expect during treatment. However, if CBT is evaluated to be inappropriate for your situation, or you do not feel comfortable with the process, you should work with your therapist to determine alternative treatments.

Further CBT sessions

Once you are through with the first session, start working with your therapist to break down your problem into various parts. To help you through this phase, your therapist will ask to keep a diary and notes on your behavioral patterns and thoughts, as well as their assessment of your progress.

During this time, you will both analyze what your thoughts, feelings and actions are like so that you can determine whether they are realistic and helpful when faced with a situation. The main aim of this analysis is to enable you to accurately determine what effects they have on you and each other. Then your therapist will help you work out ways in which you can change these thoughts and behaviors to improve your situation.

Once you know what you can change, you will have to practice the tips daily. Some of these include questioning thoughts that are upsetting and then replacing them with helpful ones; and recognizing when you are about to respond in a manner likely to make the situation worse rather than better.

To help with this exercise, it may be important to do homework sessions to help improve the process. Otherwise, during each session, it is important that you discuss with your therapist ways in which you have been able to practice these tips and come up with suggestions to help you further.

Remember that confronting your fears and anxieties can be tough, but your therapist will not ask you to do anything that you do not want to do. In other words, they will work at your pace so that you are comfortable with and during the sessions and the progress you are making. Once you are through with your sessions, the good thing is that you can keep applying principles that you learned to your daily life, hence lowering the chances of your symptoms recurring.

3 CHAPTER

TYPES OF COGNITIVE BEHAVIOR THERAPY

As mentioned earlier, it is evident that CBT utilizes some different approaches in addressing specific problems affecting people. Some of the types of CBT include:

Rational emotive behavior therapy (REBT)

This type of CBT is mainly focused on identifying any irrational beliefs that the patient might have and then trying to alter them. The process is characterized by first identifying the underlying source of the irrational beliefs, then actively challenging them and eventually learning ways to recognize and change these thoughts.

Cognitive therapy

This is a form of CBT that is mainly concerned with the identification of any distorted thought patterns, behaviors, and emotional responses; and then changing them.

Multimodal therapy

This is also a form of CBT that emphasizes that treatment of any psychological issue involves addressing seven distinct modalities that are interconnected with each other. These modalities include: affect, behavior, imagery, sensation, interpersonal factors, cognition, and biological aspects.

Dialectical Behavior Therapy (DBT)

This is also a variant of CBT that mainly pays attention to thought processes and behaviors of an individual by integrating such strategies as emotional intelligence and mindfulness in addressing them.

CHAPTER 4

ONE THING FUELING YOUR ANXIETY AND DEPRESSION

Anxiety and depression can be incredibly debilitating. It can suck the fun out of everything, leaving you an empty shell worried sick the entire night and day. You are left sweating, having stomach cramps and experiencing a recurring negative cycle of more and more anxiety each time.

But the real question here is 'what is that one thing that fuels your anxiety and depression?' Well, it's negative thoughts! Everything is a result of your thoughts. Your perception of every situation has an impact on how hard and frequent your vibrations are.

The main issue with depression is the fact that your reality becomes distorted. The things that you used to find enjoyable are all of a sudden less fun. In other words, you simply have a hard time seeing the positive aspects of your life. Your mind latches on to and cycles through negative thoughts repeatedly until you are convinced that the worst is true!

You simply feel a strong voice telling you that you cannot make it; it is your fault and so on. What is disturbing is the fact that it is very hard to challenge these beliefs. This is not just because your thoughts tell you that they are true, but also because you might already be deep in the situation making it seem true.

One thing that you have to tell yourself is: *perception does not equal reality!*

The first thing that you have to do is to set aside anxiety for a moment. Realize that even people who are successful and do not suffer anxiety often experience a disconnect between reality and their perception. One of the biggest tricks that the brain plays on you is convincing you that everyone around you is successful and talented but you.

It is this trick that takes away your motivation and passion that is fundamental in fighting off all distortions. Note that people who do not suffer from anxiety often feel as though they are fake, but they keep reminding themselves that this is all in the head and all others around them feel the same. However, since you are suffering from anxiety and depression, doing the same can be challenging.

Ten years ago, I was depressed, and every time my circumstances changed, and I had evidence for the contrary, I found myself holding on to the worst-case scenario of myself. Indeed, that was what the brain wanted me to believe. The truth is, it did not matter how much validation I got or whom it was coming from. It is a hard fact to bear in mind.

The point is, your thoughts are playing a trick on you, only that you are falling for it. Therefore, rather than allowing your thoughts to steer your life to a dark pit of fear and frustration, take a moment to tell yourself that even though you think something about yourself, that does not mean that it is true.

Your thoughts fuel three types of energies that make you feel stressed. These energies include:

a) Sensitive energy anxiety

Did you know that people with high levels of empathy struggle with anxiety? Well then now you know. If this is you, the truth is that you probably are invaded by the energy of others often.

In most cases, this kind of energy feels like a metal overload. In other words, you become overly anxious because you are overwhelmed by what you are picking up from the people around you.

To get rid of this sensitive energy anxiety, one thing that you have to think about is the amount of time you spend in social gatherings. Even though you might not consider yourself an introvert, it is important that you take time to rest so that you can recharge after interacting with people.

Additionally, it is vital that you consider whether your empathy and compassion cause you to channel too much emotional energy to efforts in pursuit of meeting their needs. One thing that you have to realize is that it is okay to say "No" whenever you are overwhelmed. It is healthy for you to think about yourself first before anyone else. This way, you increase the chances of giving back twice as much to the world around you.

The point is, always have outlets for your emotions; whether it is a therapist, a friend or a journal. It is worth your while!

b) Future energy anxiety

This is the kind of anxiety in which one overthinks and has a potent imagination. What do you feel when you are faced by a situation? Does your mind feel as though it is racing a mile per second? Do you try hard to figure out what you will do for every event that happens? Do these thoughts revolve around the worst-case scenario?

If this is you, there is a high chance that your anxiety is triggered by future energy. Yes, it may be tough to deal with the fact that you cannot control everything. In fact, what is even harder is making decisions because you are not certain that what you are doing is the right thing.

However, to get to the top of your anxiety, it is important that you focus on determining the best ways that you can effectively and consistently relax your mind. When you do this, you lower the chances of getting carried away by a sea of negative thoughts.

One way to let out these negative thoughts is to engage your mind in brilliant imaginative activities such as painting, making music, and writing among others. You can also anchor yourself to the present by practicing mindfulness and meditating. This way, you can allow yourself to let go of the things that you cannot change and accept them as they are.

c) Ascension energy anxiety

This is the kind in which one feels anxious when they are trying to respond to shifting energies in their life. This is often triggered by such changes as health conditions, loss, aging and other difficulties that are beyond your control. Additionally, this can be triggered by positive changes that may come as a result of your actions and engagements such as manifestation techniques.

If you feel as though the Law of Attraction is making you anxious, trust me, you are not alone! This is simply the ascension energy in control. Therefore, the best way to deal with this depends on the type of change driving you.

The secret is for you to trust that the process of growth is significant. Accept that the Universe is causing you to shift to places where you were meant to go. It is by grounding yourself to these simple pleasures that you can learn to appreciate the changes in your life. You could also channel this energy into such helpful activities as dancing, running, and yoga, among others.

Yes, everyone experiences some sort of anxiety, but this is unique to each one of us. In some cases, it may be definitive; in others, it may be partly external and partly internal. That said, it is critical that you seek medical attention especially if this makes your life a misery. You can also try to practice self-care. However, if that does not yield positive results, seek more advice.

It may be that the condition you are experiencing can be treated by meditation or may benefit from CBT which will aim at changing your subconscious attitudes and beliefs.

CHAPTER 5

THE *"TRICKS"* YOUR MIND PLAYS THAT DISTORT YOUR REALITY AND HOLD YOU BACK

There are so many tricks that the mind plays on you and cause a distortion of reality. Some of these tricks include:

All-or-nothing thinking

This is also referred to as polarized thinking or 'black-and-white thinking.' This distortion often is seen as an inability to appreciate the shades of gray. You simply perceive things in the sense of extremes. In other words, you may see something as either a total success or a total failure.

Over-generalization

This is one of the sneaky ways in which the mind takes one instance and uses it to generalize it to get an overall pattern. For example, if you score a D in a Math test, you generalize that you are stupid and a failure. The problem is that with additional overgeneralizations, the mind conjures more negative thoughts about oneself and its surroundings just based on a single experience.

Mental filter

This is quite similar to overgeneralization except that with the mental filter, the mind chooses to focus on one single negative and excludes all other positives; however, much they are positive. For instance, in a relationship, if your partner says something negative, you choose to dwell so much on it that you do not see all the other good things they do or say.

This single instance often makes you conclude that the relationship is hopeless. In other words, the mind chooses to filter out all the positive stuff and fosters the negative view of everything around you.

Disqualification of the positive

In this case, the mind acknowledges all positive experiences and chooses to disregard them all rather than embracing them. For example, when you receive a positive review at work, you simply choose to reject it on the grounds of such issues as political correctness, or another's inability to talk about experiences with transparency.

The problem with this trick is that it facilitates a build-up of more and more negative thoughts despite all the evidence that proves the contrary.

Jumping to conclusions

This is often interpreted as a mind reading trick. It often manifests itself in the form of invalid beliefs that we are certain what the other person is thinking. Well, you may have a good idea of what could be going through another person's mind, but there is no way to know for sure.

In other words, this kind of distortion focuses on the negative assumptions that we jump to. For instance, you may meet a stranger with an unpleasant expression and conclude immediately that they do not like you when this might not even be the case.

Fortune telling

This simply refers to the tendency to draw conclusions without any prior information or evidence to support them. You simply make a prediction and preach it as the gospel truth.

For instance, you may be single now but then start believing that you will never find love or be happy. You cannot allow your mind to convince you that you will never be happy when you do not have evidence about how your life will turn out. The fact that you have no job now does not mean that you will never have one.

Magnification or minimalization

This is also referred to as catastrophizing or 'binocular trick.' The mind simply skews your perspective of things and leads you to exaggerate or minimize the meaning or importance of something. For instance, if you are a good manager, and one time you make a mistake, you start magnifying that mistake and believe that you are not fit for your role. On the other hand, in a competition, you may emerge a winner but then choose to minimize the importance of your win by still holding on to the belief that you are incompetent.

Emotional reasoning

This is often the most surprising mind distortion, yet the most important one to identify and solve. The main reason for this is the fact that we all have bought into this trick at one point in our lives.

Emotional reasoning is one of the tricks in which the mind causes us to accept our emotions as a fact! In other words, just because you feel something, you believe it as the truth!

'Should' statements

This is one of the most damaging mind tricks that we tend to fall for. They are simply those statements that you make to yourself concerning what you 'should or ought' to do or become. In other words, you impose a set of expectations on yourself or the people around you that they may likely not meet at all.

The problem is that, when we hang on too tightly to these statements and fail to live up to them, we end up with guilt and brokenness. When we expect too much of the people in our lives, and they fail to meet our expectations, we become heartbroken and disappointed. This triggers anger and resentment.

Personalization

Just as the name suggests, this involves you taking everything personally or choosing to apportion blame to yourself without any logical reason. With this kind of distortion, you end up assuming that the reason why someone else failed is because of you, the reason the party was a total fail was because of you and so on.

Labeling and Mislabeling

This is an extreme form of overgeneralization. It simply involves you assigning judgments of value to yourself or others just because of one experience. For example, just because a customer bargains a lot does not mean that they are misers.

On the other hand, mislabeling is about applying highly emotional and loaded language when labeling yourself or others.

Always being right

This is mainly a distortion that affects people who are perfectionists and those that suffer from the imposter syndrome. It is a simple belief that what we say is always right, accurate or correct. In other words, you simply believe that there is no way you can be wrong and hence, you find yourself fighting with others just to prove that you are right.

For instance, on Twitter, you will find people who argue for hours over political issues and who is wrong and who is right. In other words, you do not get to a reasonable point where you agree to disagree. This is mainly because, to you, it is not just a matter of difference in opinion; it is an intellectual fight that you must win.

Heaven's reward fallacy

This is one of the most popular kinds of distortions which manifests as a belief that your struggles, pain, and suffering will eventually result in a fair reward. Take a moment to consider how many of these distortions you can think of within your realm of personal acquaintances as far as hard work and sacrifices go? I bet that there are many!

One thing that you have to bear in mind is regardless of how hard you work or sacrifice, you may not achieve all that you hope to achieve. When you think otherwise, you end up having a potentially damaging line of thought that ends in disappointments, anger, frustrations, depression, and anxiety, especially when the long-anticipated reward does not come around.

Control fallacies

This often manifests itself in two major ways: that we have no control over our lives and that it is upon fate to determine that; or that we are in control of our lives and the world around us and hence, are responsible for what we feel.

Well, there is no better evil in this case. This is because both beliefs are rather damaging and inaccurate. The truth is, no one is fully in control of what happens to them. On the other hand, no one has zero control over their situations.

Even though in certain situations you may seem to have no choice on what to do or where to go, the fact is that you still have some amount of control especially over how you approach a situation consciously.

Fallacy change

This is the kind of trick in which the mind tells you that people will change if only you could pressure or encourage them to do so. In other words, we tend to hold on to the belief that our success and happiness relies on other people. Hence, we end up believing that unless the people around us change, we cannot achieve what we desire.

You may be thinking 'if only I could encourage my husband to work harder, I can be a better wife and have a happy marriage.' Trust me, you are just exhibiting a fallacy of change. You cannot always count on others for your happiness. You have to begin to turn that around and take charge of your own happiness and satisfaction.

Fallacy of fairness

Inasmuch as we would love to operate in a world that is just, this ideal is not based on reality. It can simply foster negative thoughts and feelings when we face something that proves to us that life can be unfair sometimes.

Therefore, instead of judging every experience by what is and what is not just, choose to embrace things as they are. Otherwise, you might become a victim of resentment, anger, and hopelessness when the inevitable finally happens.

CHAPTER 6

HOW TO IMPROVE THE LIKELIHOOD THAT YOU WILL RESPOND POSITIVELY IN THE FUTURE

Indeed, there are so many effective therapies that you can use to address your depression and anxiety. However, the good thing is that there are some strategies that you can choose to practice to improve your chances of responding to situations positively.

Some of these strategies include:

Practicing positive self-assurance

One thing that you have to realize is that anxiety can cause you to pay attention to all the negative things happening in your life. In other words, rather than looking on to ways you can use your potential to do good works, you simply dwell on how you did not handle things the right way. The problem with this kind of perspective is that it can quickly spiral into a damaging thought process that can make your anxiety and depression worse than it already is.

To avoid these negative thoughts, it is critical that you turn your attention to positive aspects of your life. This means that, when you start to worry about things that are not going well, shift your focus to the things that are going well instead. At work, you may be feeling bad about a recent interaction with your boss or colleagues. However, instead of dwelling on what did not work out, try and think of those interactions that go well and what you can learn from them to improve future interactions.

Keeping an anxiety journal

When you are depressed and anxious, one thing is for sure; it is hard to identify what is causing your symptoms. To work this out, it is essential that you keep a journal of your experience. Whenever you feel anxious, write down all the things that are making you feel that way. Ensure that you capture your emotions, feelings, and actions.

The truth is, by just writing down your thoughts and fears, you can work through some of the situations that cause you to feel overwhelmed. Going back to your journal whenever you feel anxious or bringing it to CBT sessions plays a significant role in helping you to reflect on the common sources of your anxiety so that you can eventually work through them.

Challenging negative thoughts

Realize that when you pay attention to positive thoughts, you can easily overcome negative ones whenever you experience anxiety attacks. Having a fear of negative outcomes can quickly consume your life. Therefore, whenever you feel that negative thoughts are creeping in, try as much as you can to think of the positive outcomes you can get out of your situations, such as a travel adventure.

For instance, if you are afraid of heights and often experience sweating, nausea and an elevated heart rate, rather than dwelling on your fears, try to think about the positive things that can come of your trip and the things that you have planned to do during the trip. Think of the beauty of the place you are visiting and the beautiful people that you look forward to meeting. This way, you can quickly shift your thoughts from negative moments.

Setting up a routine

Did you know that following a routine can help you get through your daily activities with much ease? It is the one thing that will help minimize the occurrence of unanticipated triggers for your anxiety. Setting up a routine ensures that everything you set out to do is achieved by the end of the day. This in effect leaves no stone unturned, hence reducing anxiety.

It is important that your routine includes healthy meals and physical exercise so that your mental and physical health is nourished. When you establish a routine for your day to day activities, your mind will shift to the schedule and the small wins of the day, so that you will not worry about uncertainties that the day could bring.

Practicing relaxation techniques

Relaxation can differ from one individual to another. This is mainly because each one of us finds our inner peace in different activities. The good thing is that there is a wide range of techniques that you can use to calm down your anxiety. Some of these techniques include: deep breathing, yoga, and meditations.

With deep breathing, you can easily relieve the tension and restlessness that is weighing you down from the inside. Just close your eyes and focus your attention on your breathing. Take a deep breath from down your diaphragm and feel the anxiety go away.

The other trick is using meditation and yoga to ward off anxiety. These techniques have a soothing and calming effect mainly because like music, they shift your mind from what is causing your anxiety to yourself and the good things that life has to offer. Soon enough, you start feeling relaxed.

Getting some exercise

This is one of the most important parts of a healthy lifestyle. This is mainly because it has both physical and mental health benefits. When you integrate exercise into your daily routine, you are motivated and inspired to get it! You will be determined to achieve healthy goals each day no matter what stands on your way. It is the thing that will shift your focus from anxiety and channel that energy to more positive outcomes.

Practicing acceptance

You have to understand that there will always be things in life that will be out of your control. Often, these things can cause you to be anxious. Overcoming this anxiety, fear, and worries can be daunting especially with the unknown in mind. However, the thing is, when you choose to focus your thoughts on the unknown, that will not help you make changes.

The best thing is for you to identify situations that trigger your anxiety and find out whether they are under your control. If they are, then it is critical that you identify the tasks that will help you get rid of worry and anxiety and get down to doing them. However, if the answer is 'no,' it is critical that you realize that not everything that happens in life is within our control. Always remind yourself that there are situations that you may not be able to change and that is okay.

CHAPTER 7

THE EASIEST WAY TO IDENTIFY YOUR PROBLEMS AND ISSUES INSTANTLY

One thing that you have to understand is that anxiety problems are not very easy to identify. This is mainly because there is extreme excitation of these worries that impact one's personality traits. In older adults, there is the frequent occurrence of fatigue, headaches and GIT distress. The worst thing is that anxiety disorders often occur concurrently with other disorders that yield symptoms that are similar to anxiety. It is because of these concurrent disorders that detection and identification can be quite a challenge.

The major difference between anxiety and normal worry is perceived distress and the ability to function. Even though serious anxiety often interferes with one's functionality, there is a good chance that mild anxiety may not be apparent unless you apply CBT with a professional therapist to probe for more information.

It is important that you tell your therapist about different factors that may be causing concern. The truth is, signs of pathological anxiety are inconsistency and painful fear and the conflict between what is perceived to be reality and actual reality.

Some of the ways that you can identify your problems include:

d) Physical complaints

Because older adults are highly likely to report physical causes of anxiety symptoms, some of the things that you should look out for include chest pains and shortness of breath. These are very critical because they overlap with medical conditions and it is important to narrow them down.

e) Eating habits

When you are anxious, there is a high likelihood that you may start developing eating disorders. In other words, you may find yourself overeating to calm yourself down, hence gaining weight. On the other hand, you may under-eat and end up losing weight.

f) Sleep patterns

If you are anxious, there is a significant chance that your sleep patterns may be altered. Many people avoid sleeping just so that they can avoid their fears. Others may stay awake imagining exaggerated dangers or so that they can avoid having bad dreams.

g) Extra-interests and hobbies

So many people diagnosed with anxiety problems and depression tend to pull away from activities that were once fun. They end up with fewer activities that they draw pleasure from because they are more fearful.

Additionally, they prefer staying back at home just to avoid facing their fears. In fact, because of the lack of hobbies to help them relax their minds and draw their thoughts away from their worries and anxieties, they end up using drugs and other illegal substances. This is because they are trying hard to avoid staying frightened at all costs.

h) Social isolations

This is one of the major signs of anxiety and depression. Well, by social isolation, I do not mean living alone. It simply means being cut off from the rest of the world. You may be living alone, but if you have friends, go out and have a wide range of activities that you engage in during your free time, you are perfectly fine.

However, 'socially isolated people' refers to those who have lost their relationships, human touch, and interaction with their friends and family. They also do not engage in any hobbies or activities that interest them and apart from leaving their home to the grocery store, the only other option for interpersonal contact is when they are seeing their therapist.

There are many reasons why people become socially isolated. For some of them it's because they suffer from certain physical problems while others are isolated because they are depressed and feel frightened to leave their homes. Often, such people end up trapped in a vicious cycle.

If you are this kind of person, you have to understand that keeping to yourself will not help address your issue. This is an indicator that you need help. Social interactions and activities are some of the things that will help lift your spirit, cheer you up and calm your fears.

Do not allow your anxiety, worry, and fears to get the best of you. Do not allow that fear to strip away the best parts and years of your life. Rather than locking yourself up in the house and pitying yourself from dawn to sunset, get up and think about the things that will help you most. For once, think about what you are missing out on.

Locking yourself up will only get your thoughts trapped in more isolation, and hence, trigger more anxiety and depression. Breaking the vicious cycle of isolation can challenging, but you have to be ready, willing, and courageous to reach out to the world around you and draw support from the people that love you most: your family and friends.

CHAPTER 8

HOW TO AVOID COGNITIVE DISTORTIONS, GENERALIZATIONS, AND "BLACK AND WHITE" WAYS OF THINKING

There are many ways in which you can avoid cognitive distortions. You can achieve this through a mix of exercises and strategies that are effective in changing your negative thought pattern to a positive way of thinking. These include such exercises as:

Reflecting on your thoughts

Self-assessment is something that you can never go wrong with as long as you avoid obsessive self-judgment. This is because of the fact that every time you notice cognitive distortions of your thoughts, you *can choose* to register them by being more conscious of them.

One way you can achieve this is by keeping a record of those thoughts so that you can study the variations or similarities between them. You have to understand that you have no reason to think that you are not lucky. The idea is for you to rationalize these assumptions and stop them every time they occur.

Question yourself

Even though you may not be accustomed to questioning yourself, it is critical that you exercise that option regularly. When you question your own opinion, you are making sure that it is not founded on cognitive distortions. This practice ensures that you do not internalize falsehoods about various situations you encounter.

Try to listen to other people's opinions

When you listen to what others think and get their perspective on things, you are in effect enriching your view of life. As a result, you will allow those cognitive distortions to disappear, and you can view the world more objectively.

Look out for information from reliable sources

Before you can start blaming others or yourself for things that go wrong, try to contrast the information you have with as many reliable sources as possible. This is one way in which you can avoid catastrophizing situations.

Develop a critical thinking

As far as anxiety is concerned, one thing that you have to bear in mind is that it is never too late to think more analytically. When you do, you will realize that your perspective of various situations becomes more holistic. In other words, you do not allow yourself to get carried away only by obvious data. Therefore, when something happens, rather than jumping into conclusions, you take a step back to analyze the merits and demerits of certain actions before you can make a decision.

Seek advice from your loved ones

Most often, it can be easy to get carried away by situations and cognitive distortions. Rather than allowing that to happen, it is essential that you approach every situation with someone that you trust. This way, you can have a different perspective and ensure that you are objective.

Indeed, it is not easy to deal with cognitive distortions. However, one thing that you should never forget is how much pain these errors in reasoning bring and try as much as you can empathize with yourself and those going through the same problems. The truth is, anyone can have anxiety problems at any given time. When you become overly critical of yourself or others, you increase pressures and anger, which will likely make the situation worse.

Here are some practical tips that you can take into account to avoid cognitive distortions:

It is possible to change your way of thinking

The unfortunate situations that we face in our lives have the potential of changing who we are. Yes, some of these situations may be worse and are hard to erase from our memory, but you have to realize that we cannot change what has happened in the past. You can choose to wear a different attitude so that you can approach situations differently in the future.

Getting rid of cognitive distortions requires effort, perseverance and desire. Every time you feel a negative thought crossing your mind, challenge it with a positive argument that contradicts it. When you do this, you end up adopting a more beneficial point of view.

Watch your language

How we express ourselves verbally weights our thoughts and behaviors. It influences our beliefs. It is easy to get caught up in language that is negative and demeaning, which can make the situation even worse. Rather than using negative language, choose to turn to positives, words that exude optimism rather than a pessimistic attitude. When you change these expressions, you will begin to see yourself as competent, hence boosting your well-being and outlook.

Keep mentally healthy habits

Your mental health is equally as important as your physical health. Both are critical to ensuring that your well-being is complete. Certain habits will ensure that you are taking good care of yourself and that you are guarding your thoughts against anything damaging and destructive.

Rather than dwelling on what did not work out, develop a strong interpersonal and emotional intelligence. Do not try to be something that you are not. Choose to see yourself for who you are so that you can edify your being with what makes you better. Eat well, have a good rest, and continually train your cognitive skills. Ensure that whatever the situations may be, you engage in activities that make you happy.

CHAPTER 9

HOW TO BOOST YOUR SELF-ESTEEM NATURALLY TO LOOK AT YOUR LIFE FROM A POSITIVE PERSPECTIVE

Did you know that your self-esteem is what gives you confidence, hence is a cornerstone to proper mental health? If you do not believe in yourself, there is no way other people will believe in you. The good news is that there are several strategies that you can use to boost your self-esteem. Some of these mental hacks include:

Pushing through self-limiting beliefs

Our thoughts sometimes are like those of a child – we think that we can conquer the world. However, when we get in touch with our adult life, we realize that our dreams, enthusiasm and beliefs become crushed.

This is when the people around us tend to superimpose their beliefs on us. They control what we can and cannot do with our lives – and that can be frustrating!

Rather than getting trapped in what other people want for your life, it is critical that you determine your own limits. The best way you can achieve this is by putting yourself out there into different situations. In other words, do not live trapped in another person's image of life for you. Instead, push through the uncomfortable. This will not only help you regain your self-esteem but will help you gain confidence and a different perspective on yourself. The truth is, you will be amazed at what you can accomplish!

Never mix up memory with facts

It is essential to understand the fact that our memory does not store up information in the same way it is presented to us. Our human nature causes us to extract the gist of a whole encounter or incident and then store the information in ways that make sense to us. This explains the reason why people who witness the same event often have quite distinct variations of the same.

In the same way, the brain tends to have a built-in confirmation bias. In other words, the brain chooses to store only information that is consistent with what we believe, the values we hold and what reflects our self-image. It is this kind of selective memory that helps the brain keep us from overloading ourselves with excess information.

It is, therefore, critical that you realize that your memory does not at all times offer you accurate information. For instance, if you are struggling with low self-esteem, the brain tells you that you do not have confidence, and hence chooses to store that information and that will be all that you recall about an event.

The trick here is for you to revisit the facts that are loaded in your memory so that you can discover all the self-limiting beliefs stored there. Then try as much as you can to gain a more accurate mindset of the event. Talk to other people with a different point of view so that you can edify your perception and change your perspective.

Talk to yourself

You may think of this as being crazy but trust me, this works magic! When you are struggling with low self-esteem, talking to yourself and changing your point of view of yourself can help. It can make you see yourself as smarter, hence boosting your memory and helping you pay closer attention to increasing your intellectual performance.

For instance, when you talk to yourself, you are in effect instructing your mind to be mentally tough and to speak positive things. This can override your fears, hence altering your limbic system, the primal part of the brain that plays a critical role in helping us deal with anxiety.

The most important thing here is for you to be positive in the manner in which you talk to yourself. This is because it has a way of influencing your neurobiological response. When you tell yourself how to do something or choose to shift your mind on various approaches to addressing a problem, you simply have turned your response to a positive one.

Think positive so that you can overcome your negativity biases

Since we were little children, we learned how to get something or be something. It is the negative bias that we possess that has successfully kept us from danger for so many years. However, what we fail to realize is that not everything that comes our way is a threat that calls for survival responses. It is this negativity bias that gradually strips us of our self-confidence mainly because we are hardwired to believe that we have done something wrong.

Professionals are trained to do good things for the company and the client. However, this can be difficult sometimes because the positive information presented to us easily falls away, while the negative information tends to stick like Velcro.

If you are going to recharge your self-esteem, it is important that you come up with at least five positive thoughts every time you have a negative thought. Allow each positive thought to sink into your spirit before progressing to the next positive thought.

Additionally, learn to acknowledge both the good and the bad emotion you feel rather than trying to suppress the negative ones. Labeling emotions for what they truly are allows you to move on. Rather than getting into an inner dialogue about the bad emotions, choose to dwell on the positive ones to win back your power.

Raise your curiosity

Being curious is one of the important traits that we human beings have. It is what makes us successful and confident in what we do. It is considered to be the foundation of life-long growth and progression. Therefore, if we maintain our curiosity, we become teachable, and this causes both our hearts and minds to grow bigger each day.

Yes, we may retain our beginner's orientation, but we can look forward to new things and experiences that uncover new information for us. To win back your self-confidence, purposefully ask questions and be curious about them. This will make your mind active, encourage you to be more observant, create new ideas, open a world of new possibilities and create a person that is full of adventure, hence guiding you into a new world of happiness and satisfaction.

Overcome self-doubt

If you do not have self-esteem and confidence, there is a good chance that you will feel as though you are at the mercy of other people. By assuming that you are a victim, you give away your resilience to roadblocks and the unavoidable things that life brings.

When you have your self-esteem, you will go where you are needed and not where you are comfortable. In other words, you will break out of your *comfort zone*. You may face challenging situations along the way that you have no idea how to solve, but you will not allow fear and panic to get the best of you. This is because you believe that no matter what, you will come out victorious on the other side.

Understand that no one but yourself is stopping you from accomplishing your dreams. Therefore, rather than blaming people for your undoing, take the time to identify areas of your life where you have doubt and then work towards getting rid of those barriers.

Stay and face your fears

Did you know that every time you feel you are in control you also are not afraid? The truth is, when we are comfortable with something, we are not scared of anything. However, when we feel as though our control is taken from us, we fail to think clearly. This is mainly because the emotional brain has shifted into the driver's seat and is suddenly is the one leading the way. This explains the reason why fear is random yet so irrational.

To feel safe and in control, it is important that we learn how to move closer to the threat. In other words, face the thing that is causing us fear. It is no good avoiding or ignoring our fears. Allow yourself to think about your fears. Spend time with your fears and make it even worse by sticking closer to them.

What is the worst that could happen? While close to your fears, focus on your breathing and allow your body to relax as much as you can. You did not die, right? Practicing facing your fears ensures that you are one step closer to overcoming those fears each time.

If you fail to believe in yourself, the truth is, other people will not reciprocate a belief in you either.

CHAPTER 10

HOW TO SET AND ACHIEVE YOUR OWN GOALS FOR BETTER LONG-TERM MENTAL HEALTH

One of the greatest challenges that many people with anxiety problems face is how to set and achieve their goals so that they enjoy better mental health in their future. This is mainly because there is no way to predict how the brain naturally works. The brain naturally tries to prioritize and choose routines over trying out new things, and this makes lots of sense because the brain's main aim is to keep you safe.

When you are trying to make changes in thoughts and behavior, the brain tries hard to settle on habitual responses rather than goal-oriented actions. This simply means that every goal that requires a radical behavior or thought process are met with lots of resistance at first.

On the other hand, the brain is wired to want to get rewards while avoiding pain, fear, anxiety, and discomfort. The thing is, this does not mean that if there is more comfort in your path, it should not interest you. It only means that that is what the brain prefers. It is these preferences that act as demotivators, and they only cause you to want to get back to your comfort zone.

However, with a conscious effort, there is a strong chance that you can override these emotional feelings and cause that to alter your brain and behavior.

Some of the ways you can set and achieve these goals in the long-term include:

Having a dopamine boost

Whenever you achieve what you have been working hard for, the brain offers you a dopamine shot. Dopamine is simply referred to as the 'feel good' hormone. Because of this, it is possible to set goals and achieve them with a dopamine boost.

For example, if you promise yourself that you are going to exercise and lose weight, then the brain gives you a dopamine boost when you achieve the goal. This explains the reason why so many people like to have a to-do list with them. It feels great to check things off your list. Therefore, every time your brain gets a shot of dopamine, it encourages you to continue with the same behavior to get a reward over and over again.

One thing you should bear in mind is that when you break those goals, you will keep the dopamine from flowing. If you want to adopt a keto diet for at least a month, you can check off your small wins with a marker on a calendar. This simply tells the brain how to see things and register each time there is an accomplishment. On the other hand, if you would like to write a book, all you have to do is set a goal to write at least 30 minutes each day and offer yourself a reward once you do.

Improved performance

According to research, the desire for improved performance is one of the driving forces for setting goals and working hard towards achieving them. All you have to do is to ensure that the goals you set are specific and challenging enough. Also, it is important that you have adequate ability and give feedback to yourself to demonstrate progress toward the goals.

When a goal is attained, rewards should be given. These rewards can take the form of money or assets. If there is a therapist, friend or family involved, it is important that they are supportive.

Use valuable experiences

Did you know that setting goals can offer you valuable experiences and the reverse is also true? The truth is, the situations that you experience are unique to you in their way, and they carry valuable lessons that you can learn from. Rather than dwelling on the negative aspects of an event, you can choose to draw lessons that will benefit your mental health in the long-term.

Valuable experiences can be the reason why you are able to learn how to be independent, resilient, kind, forgiving, and competitive among other values. These key skills go a long way in contributing to your mental health and ultimate happiness.

CHAPTER 11

PROVEN, POWERFUL, AND PRACTICAL STRATEGIES FOR OVERCOMING OBSTACLES TO AVOID A RELAPSE INTO POOR MENTAL HEALTH

If you are struggling with anxiety, just like other mental health conditions, you will experience good times and bad times. The good times are simply when your symptoms are under control, and you feel strong. On the other hand, when you are in bad times, you experience challenging setbacks, and your symptoms are worse.

These setbacks are often referred to as 'relapses.' In most cases, if they are very serious, this can lead to hospitalization. The truth is, relapses happen even though one may already be under medication.

Therefore, it is important that you develop skills that will help you cope so that you can deal with these challenges more subtly and effectively possible. In most cases, certain triggers such as situations or behaviors can cause a relapse. Knowing your trigger(s) helps you develop strategies to help you deal with them and lower your risk of a relapse.

Some of the proven ways that have been shown to help in overcoming obstacles to avoid a relapse contributing to poor mental health include:

Practice as much as you can

The best way in which one can prevent the occurrence of relapse is to keep practicing CBT skills as much as they can. This is because, when you practice regularly, you ensure that you stay in shape and hence when a situation arises, you are capable of facing it hands-on.

You can fit in practice by simply making a schedule for the skills you would like to work on each week. Some of the techniques that you can practice regularly may include exposure, relaxation, calm breathing and others. You can get friends and family to support you in maintaining your schedule.

Know what your red flags are

If you know what triggers your fears and anxiety, there is a better chance that you can spot them from afar. In other words, when you are more vulnerable to experiencing a trigger, you become self-aware, and this makes it less likely to occur.

The best thing in such a case is for you to make a list of all the warning signs that tell you that you are likely to be having an anxiety attack. Some of these might include feeling sweaty, feeling anxious, having too many responsibilities at work or home, engaging in an argument or going through major life changes.

When you are aware of the red flags, you can make a plan of action. This will ensure that you have the situation under control. In other words, reliance on a plan is your coping mechanism. Your plan may include taking a break from work, practicing relaxation and CBT skills.

Coming up with new challenges

You have to understand that, just like everyone else in the Universe, you are not perfect. You are simply a work in progress. In other words, each day is a new opportunity to improve something in your life so that you can make it more fulfilling and enjoyable.

To prevent future relapses, it is important that you keep working on new challenges and situations that make you fearful in your life. The best approach is for you to make a list of all situations that you find scary and work on each one at a time. This way, there is less chance that you will slide back to old habits. The brain will shift focus from older habits to establishing new ones and learning how to cope with new dangers, fears, and worries.

Learn a lesson or two from your relapses

It is normal to have a relapse occasionally! Every day, we face new situations, some of which are not stressful while others *are* stressful. If you are struggling with anxiety issues, coping with such events can make you more vulnerable to relapse.

However, the good news is that you can learn from the relapses that you have had in the past. Use your past experiences to figure out what the situation was that caused you to relapse.

The best way to get clarity on this is by asking yourself these questions:

- Did you have angry and anxious thought patterns?
- Was the level of your anxiety high?
- What did you do?
- Was there something that you did each time differently?
- Were you aware that the situation would be difficult or was it a surprise?

Knowing how and why your previous relapse was difficult can be useful in helping you prepare for the next one. Ensure that you have plans that will help you cope effectively in the future.

Know your facts

Did you know that what you say to yourself after having a relapse has a great impact on how you react, respond or behave? When you have had a relapse, it is important that you focus on what is helpful to you. Rather than thinking that you are a failure, think of the lessons that you can learn to make it better the next time.

This is because, when you see yourself as a failure, you will feel as though you have undone all the good work. This simply strips you of your self-confidence, driving you into giving up, hence making you relapse.

However, with some of these facts, you can ensure that everything is under control. These facts include knowing that it is impossible to go back to the starting point. In other words, accepting that you cannot unlearn all the skills and techniques that CBT has taught you. Realize that, if you went back to the starting point, there is an increased chance that you will go into relapse and not know how to handle the situation. However, once you have started CBT, you are certain that if relapse occurred in the future, you are fully equipped to handle it.

If you encounter another relapse, you have the potential to get back on track. The truth is, you might have taken weeks or even months to practice CBT techniques that help you reduce anxiety symptoms, but it will not take you an eternity to figure out how to get back on track before you encounter another episode. Understand that when you keep practicing your CBT skills, you stand a better chance of mastering your anxiety each time.

Just think of it as riding a bike. It takes time to learn, but once you know how, you are good to go, and that skill sticks with you forever. If you stop riding for a while, you get rusty, but it will not be long before you get back on track.

Be kind to yourself

It is important that you bear in mind that relapses are normal. So many people beat themselves up or demean themselves because they just had an episode. You have to understand that by blaming yourself, you are just making it even worse than it already is. Realize that just like anybody else, you are not perfect and that mistakes are bound to happen from time to time.

Ask yourself, if it were someone else having a relapse, would you speak to them the same way you are doing to yourself? Probably not! Trust me when I tell you that it can be helpful to have a relapse. I know this might sound crazy but hear me out; having a relapse gives you an opportunity to learn that relapses are not only normal but they also help a lot in overcoming triggers the next time they occur. This is mainly because you will have learned skills that help you tackle the situation and move forward with your life.

Celebrate your wins

Overcoming situations that challenge your fears, anxiety, and worry is commendable. It is very important that you take the time to appreciate yourself for the progress and hard work you are doing. When you treat yourself after every win, however small it may seem to you, you become motivated to tackle even bigger situations.

The reward can be something like treating yourself to a nice meal, buying that beautiful jewelry you have meant to, going out with your family or friends, or just enjoying pampering yourself. The truth is, managing anxiety is hard work and the progress you make is because of the effort that you put in. Think about, isn't that worth a reward?

That said, for you to overcome your anxiety and fear, it is important that you plan well for a relapse. It is important that you do the planning ahead of time so that you can have all the support and help you might need.

When you plan, you ease your worries about what might happen if you were to have an episode. This is mainly because you know that you have a plan in place in case you need it.

Plans may be formal agreements between you and your therapist. They can also be informal understandings between you and your friends, family or other people within your support network. Whatever form you choose, remember that the most important thing for you is to outline clearly what might happen, the warning signs and what each person's responsibility will be.

Others need to know the signs that indicate a relapse is about to happen. It is important that the plan also identifies the point at which outside help is needed. Is it soon after the red flags begin to show or is it the time when you can no longer manage the symptoms of your anxiety by yourself?

The plan should also entail directives about where to go for help in case you are alone or with unfamiliar people. In other words, who are your first points of contact if an emergency happened? Also, include the treatment you would prefer to have administered within such a situation.

Your action plan can also include all the practical steps that your support network agreed to take. For instance, your loved ones may be required to contact your employer so that everything is kept in order: from the rent to bill payments and other formal financial tasks, especially if you need to spend more time in the hospital.

What if you have children and this happens? Well, children need care, so a guardian's access to finances is important. It is best to seek a lawyer's advice so that you know what options you have. The good news is that there are many legal procedures and tools at your disposal that will facilitate planning for your children's care. When you work with a legal professional, you will get the best advice on what choices suit your situation.

CHAPTER12

EMOTIONAL SELF-AWARENESS

You may be thinking 'What does this have to do with my anxiety issues?' Well, trust me, it has everything to do with resolving anxiety! Emotional awareness is all about being able to recognize and understand your emotions and how they affect or influence your behavior.

We have already seen how anxiety issues or occurrence of a situation that triggers your anxiety issues and fear can trigger a relapse and the various ways in which you can avoid that from happening. However, during the process, there are so many emotional changes that take place, and if you are going to respond well to situations, you have to be aware of your emotions.

The good thing is that you know how you feel and the reasons why you feel that way. This simply means that you can see how your emotions can be helpful or hurtful to what you do. In such a situation, there is also a chance that you are aware of how people view you. But there is a huge difference between emotional intelligence and cognitive self-awareness, which mainly pays attention to your thoughts and ideas instead of your feelings.

Emotional intelligence is one of the core competencies that help you manage your emotions, relationships, and awareness of others. Next, we will discuss the various steps that you can follow to help you develop awareness of your feelings and how they are interconnected with your thoughts.

Step 1: Choose a triggering situation

By now, you already know the things that trigger anger, anxiety and upsetting feelings for you. Try to put them down on paper and select one that is least challenging to you just for starters. The reason why we begin with the least challenging is so that you can practice your skills successfully one at a time until you can face your worst fears.

This may take days to weeks, hence the need for patience. Try to stretch yourself out of your comfort zone while still ensuring that you do not get overwhelmed in the process. However, if you feel that this process is emotionally overwhelming, it is important that you seek help from someone that can work with you – like a therapist, friend or family member.

Step 2: Center yourself in the present while taking in slow and deep breaths

Once you know what trigger you would like to work on, it is important that you pause for a moment and close your eyes. Take in slow and deep breaths for about 5-10 minutes. Breath from your belly and allow your whole body to come to the point of relaxation.

Focus your mind on your breath with your eyes closed. In your mind, scan your body from head to toe allowing every tension to be released. Let loose every tightness in your body so that you relax.

Now, start imagining yourself at a safe place. Try to remind yourself that you are not the emotions or the thoughts but just an observer and a person that can choose the thoughts and emotions that appeal to you. How does that make you feel? Do you feel that you are in charge of your body, responses, thoughts, and feelings? Imagine not having anyone around you making you feel what you do not want to without your permission. You are simply the observer of your emotional feelings.

Now, start shifting your mind into creating a mental note to yourself. In this note, tell yourself that the emotions you are experiencing are old energy pockets, wounds that come from your past experiences, and your childhood. Tell yourself that this is okay because, during that time, you had no cognitive ability to know or even see yourself from different points of view. Now, you have become an intelligent adult who is well able to take charge of all processes and changes taking place in your life.

Repeat it over and over until your brain gets a positive attitude towards your inner and outer person.

If you need to stop this exercise in the middle of it at any time, you can do so if necessary, otherwise, ensure that you can do it to the end without any interruptions.

Step 3: Identify and feel your emotions

While feeling centered in your breathing, start to bring that trigger into your mind. You can do this by simply trying to recall the latest/most recent occurrence. Avoid making any judgments and pause for a moment to get in touch with your feelings and sensations. Take note of any emotions and feelings you had inside.

Now, try to take deep and slow breaths while still feeling what you felt when you had the occurrence. Begin to ask yourself what you are feeling at that moment. Do you feel anger? Do you feel scared? Are you anxious? Start looking for the emotions that run beneath it. Anger is but a secondary emotion that comes on as a means of trying to protect yourself from feeling vulnerable.

Is there something that underlies that anger? Is it hurt, shame, fear or something else? What emotional feelings do you have? Write them down on a plain sheet of paper or in a journal.

Step 4: Feel and take note of the location of sensations in your body

At this point, it is critical that you take a moment, pause and feel each emotion run through your body. Take note of the sensations that you feel at different parts of your body. For each of the emotions that is triggered, record the sensation that you feel and what part of the body you feel it in. You can do this by ensuring that you maintain the picture of your triggering event in your mind.

Ensure that while you're at it, you take in deep breaths and place your hand(s) on the place where you feel the sensation. As you do this, begin to let go of any impulse that pulls you towards judging, stopping, repressing or fixing your emotions and sensations. Keep probing your emotions and taking note of the emotional feelings until they lessen in intensity.

If you feel that anger is primary, keep asking yourself whether there is something other than anger that you are feeling. Give a description of your sensations and the body parts where you feel them. Record them and keep repeating this until you have exhausted all the primary emotions.

Step 5: Accept your feelings and have the confidence that you can handle your emotions and sensations

Here, it is important that you keep reminding yourself that your emotions do not define who you are. You are not your emotions but just an observer of your emotions. Tell yourself that those emotions that you have are energy, and your feelings are pockets or charged energy that is associated directly with your past pains and wounds.

In other words, as a choice maker for your life, you have the free-will to choose what you want. You can breathe into painful, fearful and anxious situations. As you do that, notice those sensations, and emotional feelings shift, move away and allow yourself to release them. Affirm to yourself that you have the power to accept these feelings as they are at that very moment.

Start telling yourself that you can handle it. Tell yourself that you are strong enough to handle the situation with ease, calm and wisdom. Realize that one of the most powerful leverages that you have over negative emotions is reminding yourself about the time you had them and how you handled them successfully.

In other words, if you have been able to handle this well in the past, there is a strong possibility that you can handle it again in the present and future. Tell yourself that you have done so in the past and you can do it again and again in the future. Keep repeating the affirmations as many times as you possibly can or until you experience a smooth shift of emotional state and intensity.

Allow yourself to take in slow and deep breaths throughout the body and in between the repetitions. Bear in mind that every time you handle the emotion, you add that into your repertoire of success. This will eventually grow and strengthen your confidence as well as your ability to handle similar situations in the future. This will allow you to pick up lessons that will help you turn fear-based emotions into assets.

Step 6: Identify what you tell yourself in your mind that triggers pain

Now, start taking note of your thoughts as you picture the triggering event. Record any toxic thoughts and feelings that come through your mind. The truth is, what you think often triggers an emotional feeling and physical sensations in your body. This is just how the brain functions.

All you have to do here is to watch those thoughts from afar. Remember that you are not the emotion or the thoughts; you are simply an observer that is taking note of things as they happen without making any judgments.

Whenever you get disturbing thoughts, imagine riding in a luxurious train that is speeding. Imagine that you are looking out the window taking note of every thought or emotion that causes anger and then quickly close the window as you get back to your comfortable seat; your safe place.

Record everything that you tell yourself while you have that self-talk adjacent to the emotions and physical sensations you experienced.

Step 7: Empathetically connect so that you can understand and validate your experiences

It is important that you keep reminding yourself that even though other people or situations may trigger a painful feeling in you, they are not the cause of your pain. It is your self-talk that is causing you so much pain. It is what you tell yourself that is triggering the resentment, anger, guilt, and frustration among other emotions you may be experiencing.

It is the thing that you tell yourself that is causing the physical body sensations that you have. Well, trust me, this is good news! The main reason why I say this is because the way you explain your triggers to yourself is the cause of your emotional feelings. It is what causes you to get upset.

The thing is, you can change that. The way to do this is to choose to tell yourself something positive no matter the situation. Think thoughts that cause you to be calm, empowered and loaded with confidence. This is the best way in which you can start making informed decisions and choices.

Start making a mental note telling yourself how this is really good news. In other words, you are telling yourself that you are the one in charge of what emotional response you experience, the thoughts that you have as well as the actions that you take.

Understand that your happiness is your responsibility. For you to achieve that peace of mind irrespective of what the triggering event is, it is only you that can find it. There is no other person that can make you feel a certain way when you do not want to feel that way. You only feel what you feel because you want to.

When you allow this to sink into your spirit, you will find yourself creating statements that give affirmations that simply validate your experience. Start telling yourself 'it is okay that I feel overwhelmed' rather than telling yourself that you cannot handle it, you can never get things done or even that it is too much for you.

That said, remember that thoughts are what trigger feelings. It is then that feelings communicate important information on how you can handle your life to thrive or survive worse situations. When you grow your awareness of the emotions and sensations that you experience, you gain more understanding of the strong connection between self-talk and what you feel.

Once you do, you realize that you have so much power that you never thought you had and hence you can now regulate your emotional state as you wish. You realize that when you make small changes in your thought process, you chart the course of your life by simply making a conscious choice of how you experience different events. You simply experience situations in ways that enrich the direction that you have chosen.

Your painful emotions allow you to know whether you are on the right path to emotional fulfillment or not. Once you know the power that emotions have on shaping your life and the way they work hand in hand with your thoughts, it will be much easier to stop despising them. Just remember that in this sea of life, your navigation system is what you allow yourself to feel.

CONCLUSION

Indeed, CBT starts with a rather straightforward way in which we can understand a challenging situation and how we react to it. What you have to remember is that cognitive behavioral therapy focuses on the three major components of a psychological problem: thoughts, emotions, and behaviors.

This simply means that when you experience a challenging situation, it is important that you break it down into these components. When you break it down in this manner, you gain clarity about where to intervene and how to do it. In other words, if there is a chain of reactions of both behavior and emotional feelings that arise from having a particular negative thought, the best approach is to go back into reexamining the thought. However, if a negative pattern of behavior seems to be the main problem, the wiser thing to do is to learn a new response to the situation.

The truth is, there is no quicker way to fix your anxiety. It takes time and commitment for you to fully overcome your fears. When you go through cognitive behavioral therapy, it is important that you face your fears head-on rather than trying to run away from them. This might make you feel worse at first, but it is only after that you can start feeling better. The most important thing is for you to try as much as you can to stick to your therapy and the advice given by your therapist.

Your pace or recovery may be slow, and this can be discouraging at the time, but you have to remember that it will be effective in the long-run. Therefore, rather than giving up, keep pressing on, and you will eventually reap the benefits. To support your therapy, it is essential that you start making positive choices. This includes everything from your level of activity to your social life and how that affects your condition. The best route is for you to begin by setting goals and making informed decisions that will boost your levels of relaxation and functionality and offer you a positive mental outlook in your daily life.

Take time to learn about your anxiety so that it becomes easier to overcome it. Education is really important in ensuring that you know what it takes to get to the other side of recovery. True, that alone will not cure your condition, but it will help you make sense of your healing therapy.

Cultivate your support network so that you are not isolated and lonely, as loneliness can make your anxiety even worse. When you establish a robust system of support from your therapist, family, and friends, you will significantly lower your level of vulnerability. Make a point to see your support group frequently so that you can share with them your worries, concerns, and progress.

Also, remember to adopt a healthy lifestyle by engaging in physical activities and eating healthy foods. This regimen goes a long way in helping to achieve relaxation by relieving tension and anxiety. Therefore, in your daily routine, make it a point to schedule regular exercises. Also, refrain from foods and drinks that may make your anxiety worse such as those containing caffeine or alcohol.

"Strong feelings shape thoughts, not the other way around. You can directly help lift and calm feelings, so thoughts fall in line with calmer emotionality."

Mark Tyrrell

You may also be interested in my other books:

The Enneagram

The Ultimate Insight to Self-Awareness and Personal Growth for You

Anger Management

How to Take Self Control of Your Anger and the Ultimate Insight to Self-Awareness

Emotional and Narcissistic Abuse

The Complete Survival Guide to Understanding Narcissism, Escaping the Narcissist in a Toxic Relationship Forever, and Your Road to Recovery